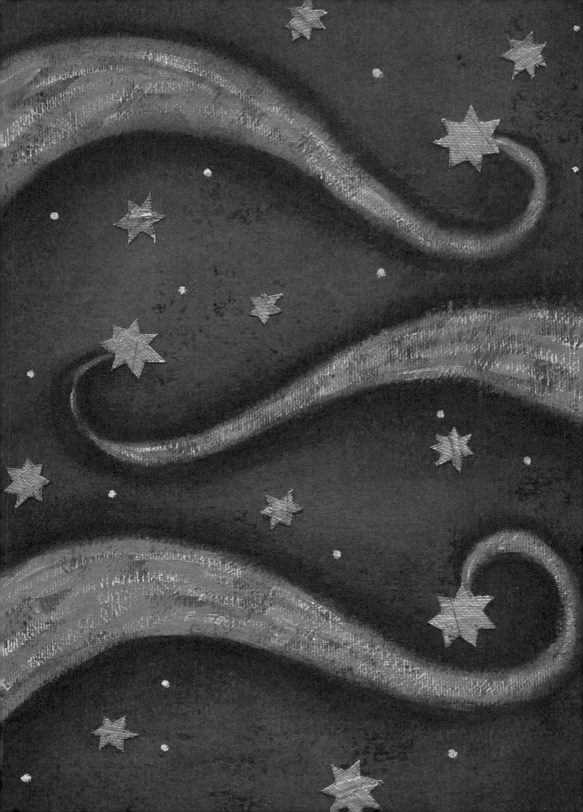

My First Hymnal

"I will sing and make melody to the Lord."

Psalm 27:6b

Name

Daisy

Date

June 13, 2019

Given by

Redeemer Lutheran Church
and
Deaconess Pat

My First Hymnal

CONCORDIA PUBLISHING HOUSE · SAINT LOUIS ·

Copyright © 2011 Concordia Publishing House
3558 S. Jefferson Ave., St. Louis, MO 63118-3968
1-800-325-3040 • cph.org

Unless otherwise indicated, Scripture quotations are from The Holy Bible,
English Standard Version ® (ESV ®), Copyright © 2001 by Crossway, a
publishing ministry of Good News Publishers. All rights reserved.

Manufactured in the United States of America
Illustrations by Paine Proffitt © Concordia Publishing House

Manufactured in Lowell, MA/036656/413474

19 20 21 22 23 24 25 26 27 28   27 26 25 24 23 22 21 20 19 18

Contents

Introduction

Hymnals contain prayers, creeds, psalms, and songs for God's people. This hymnal is designed to be a child's first hymnal—a book filled with the Church's song and with illustrations that together tell the story of Jesus and His Church.

Jesus comes into the flesh to serve us. On the cross He offered Himself to be our sacrifice for the sins of the world. Through His perfect life, ministry, death, and resurrection, Jesus gives to His children grace, mercy, forgiveness, and eternal life.

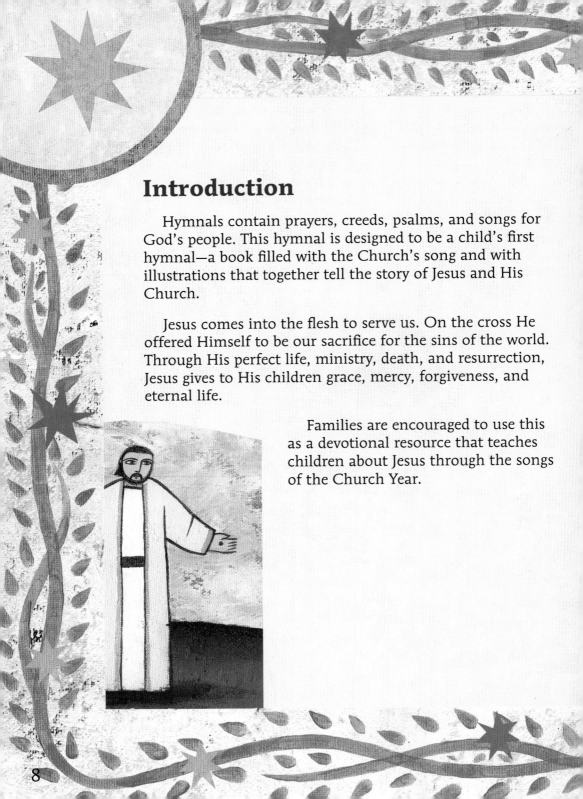

Families are encouraged to use this as a devotional resource that teaches children about Jesus through the songs of the Church Year.

Sing and make melody to
the Lord with your heart!
Ephesians 5:19b, adapted

christmas

Advent

Holy trinity

pentecost

The Church Year

The Church Year unfolds in days, weeks, months, and seasons. These seasons unpack the truth of the Holy Scriptures, which tell about the promises, life, redemption, and forgiveness we, as children, have in Jesus. Different colors, symbols, and images remind us of the mystery and holiness of God—Father, Son, and Holy Spirit.

Easter

10

Epiphany

Lent

Holy Week

11

Psalms

Children and parents gather together to pray, share, sing, and speak the poetry of God, words that promise Jesus for His children. Select verses are in bold print to encourage responsive reading.

8

O Lord, our Lord,
how majestic is your name in all the earth!

You have set your glory above the heavens.

Out of the mouth of babies and infants,
you have established strength because of your foes,
to still the enemy and the avenger.

When I look at your heavens,
the work of your fingers,
the moon and the stars,
which you have set in place,

O Lord, our Lord,
how majestic is your name in all the earth!

what is man that you are mindful of him,
and the son of man that you care for him?

Yet you have made him a little lower
    than the heavenly beings
    and crowned him with glory and honor.

You have given him dominion over
    the works of your hands;
    you have put all things under his feet,

**O LORD, our Lord,
    how majestic is your name in all the earth!**

all sheep and oxen,
    and also the beasts of the field,

the birds of the heavens, and the fish of the sea,
    whatever passes along the paths of the seas.

**O LORD, our Lord,
    how majestic is your name in all the earth!**

13

23

The Lord is my shepherd; I shall not want.

He makes me lie down in green pastures.
    He leads me beside still waters.

He restores my soul.
    He leads me in paths of righteousness
    for his name's sake.

The Lord is my shepherd; I shall not want.

Even though I walk through the valley
    of the shadow of death, I will fear no evil,
    for you are with me;
    your rod and your staff, they comfort me.

You prepare a table before me
    in the presence of my enemies;
    you anoint my head with oil; my cup overflows.

Surely goodness and mercy shall
    follow me all the days of my life,
    and I shall dwell in the house of the LORD forever.

The LORD is my shepherd; I shall not want.

46

**God is our refuge and strength,
a very present help in trouble.**

Therefore we will not fear though the earth gives way,
though the mountains be moved
into the heart of the sea,

though its waters roar and foam,
though the mountains tremble at its swelling.

There is a river whose streams make glad the city of God,
the holy habitation of the Most High.

God is in the midst of her; she shall not be moved;
God will help her when morning dawns.

**God is our refuge and strength,
a very present help in trouble.**

The nations rage, the kingdoms totter;
he utters his voice, the earth melts.

The Lord of hosts is with us;
  the God of Jacob is our fortress.

Come, behold the works of the Lord,
  how he has brought desolations on the earth.

He makes wars cease to the end of the earth;
  he breaks the bow and shatters the spear;
  he burns the chariots with fire.

"Be still, and know that I am God. I will be exalted among
  the nations, I will be exalted in the earth!"

The Lord of hosts is with us;
  the God of Jacob is our fortress.

**God is our refuge and strength,
  a very present help in trouble.**

51:1–3, 9–12

Have mercy on me, O God,
according to your steadfast love;

according to your abundant mercy
blot out my transgressions.

Wash me thoroughly from my iniquity,
and cleanse me from my sin!

For I know my transgressions,
and my sin is ever before me.

Have mercy on me, O God,
according to your steadfast love.

Hide your face from my sins,
and blot out all my iniquities.

Create in me a clean heart, O God,
and renew a right spirit within me.

Cast me not away from your presence,
and take not your Holy Spirit from me.

Restore to me the joy of your salvation,
and uphold me with a willing spirit.

Have mercy on me, O God,
according to your steadfast love.

121

I lift up my eyes to the hills.
From where does my help come?

**My help comes from the Lord,
who made heaven and earth.**

He will not let your foot be moved;
he who keeps you will not slumber.

Behold, he who keeps Israel
will neither slumber nor sleep.

**My help comes from the Lord,
who made heaven and earth.**

The Lord is your keeper;
the Lord is your shade on your right hand.

The sun shall not strike you by day,
nor the moon by night.

The Lord will keep you from all evil;
he will keep your life.

The Lord will keep your going out
and your coming in
from this time forth and forevermore.

**My help comes from the Lord,
who made heaven and earth.**

150

Praise the LORD! Praise God in his sanctuary;
  praise him in his mighty heavens!

Praise him for his mighty deeds;
  praise him according to his excellent greatness!

Praise him with trumpet sound;
  praise him with lute and harp!

Praise him with tambourine and dance;
  praise him with strings and pipe!

Praise him for his mighty deeds;
  praise him according to his excellent greatness!

Praise him with sounding cymbals;
  praise him with loud clashing cymbals!

Let everything that has breath praise the LORD!
  Praise the LORD!

Praise him for his mighty deeds;
  praise him according to his excellent greatness!

Morning Prayers

The sign of the cross ✠ may be made by all in remembrance of their Baptism.

In the name of the Father and of the ✠ Son and of the Holy Spirit.
Amen.

In the morning, O Lord, You hear my voice;
in the morning I prepare a sacrifice for You and watch.

My mouth is filled with Your praise,
and with Your glory all the day.

O Lord, open my lips,
and my mouth will declare Your praise.

Glory be to the Father and to the Son and to the Holy Spirit; as it was in the beginning, is now, and will be forever. Amen.

A portion of Scripture may be read. A hymn may be sung.

Morning

Faithful God, whose mercies are new to us every morning, we humbly pray that You would look upon us in mercy and renew us by Your Holy Spirit. Keep safe our going out and our coming in, and let Your blessing remain with us throughout this day. Preserve us in Your righteousness, and grant us a portion in that eternal life which is in Christ Jesus, our Lord. **Amen.**

Life as a baptized child of God

Merciful Father, through Holy Baptism You called us to be Your own possession. Grant that our lives may evidence the working of Your Holy Spirit in love, joy, peace, patience, kindness, goodness, faithfulness, gentleness, and self-control, according to the image of Your only-begotten Son, Jesus Christ, our Savior. **Amen.**

For guidance in a new day

Lord God, You have called Your servants to ventures of which we cannot see the ending, by paths as yet untrodden, through perils unknown. Give us faith to go out with good courage, not knowing where we go but only that Your hand is leading us and Your love supporting us; through Jesus Christ, our Lord. **Amen.**

Let us bless the Lord.
Thanks be to God.

My Maker, hold me in Your hand;
O Christ, forgiven let me stand;
Blest Comforter, do not depart;
With faith and love enrich my heart.

Lord, bless and keep me as Your own;
Lord, look in kindness from Your throne;
Lord, shine unfailing peace on me
By grace surrounded; set me free.

O Blessed, Holy Trinity, sts. 4–5

Luther's Morning Prayer

I thank You, my heavenly Father, through Jesus Christ, Your dear Son, that You have kept me this night from all harm and danger; and I pray that You would keep me this day also from sin and every evil, that all my doings and life may please You. For into Your hands I commend myself, my body and soul, and all things. Let Your holy angel be with me, that the evil foe may have no power over me. Amen.

Evening Prayers

The sign of the cross ✚ may be made by all in remembrance of their Baptism.

In the name of the Father and of the ✚ Son and
of the Holy Spirit.
Amen.

A candle may be lighted.

Let my prayer rise before You as incense,
the lifting up of my hands as the evening sacrifice.

Joyous light of glory:
of the immortal Father;
heavenly, holy, blessed Jesus Christ.
We have come to the setting of the sun,
and we look to the evening light.
We sing to God, the Father, Son, and Holy Spirit:
You are worthy of being praised
with pure voices forever.
O Son of God, O Giver of life:
the universe proclaims Your glory.

A portion of Scripture may be read. A hymn may be sung.

Evening

Merciful Father, whose guiding hand has brought us
to the completion of this day, we humbly pray You to stay with
us and shelter us in quiet hours of the night that we, who are
wearied by the changes and chances of this passing world, may
rest in Your changeless peace; through Jesus Christ, our Lord.
Amen.

Thanksgiving at end of the day

Gracious Lord, we give You thanks for the day,
especially for the good we were permitted to give and
to receive. The day is now past, and we commit it to You. We
entrust to You the night and rest in Your peace, for You are
our help, and You neither slumber nor sleep. Hear us for the
sake of Your name. **Amen.**

For protection

Visit our dwelling, O Lord, and keep all harm and
danger far from us. Grant that we may live together in peace
under the protection of Your holy angels; through Jesus Christ,
our Lord. **Amen.**

Let us bless the Lord.
Thanks be to God.

Ah, dearest Jesus, holy Child,
Prepare a bed, soft, undefiled,
A quiet chamber set apart
For You to dwell within my heart.

From Heaven Above to Earth I Come, st. 13

Jesus, Savior, wash away
All that has been wrong today;
Help me ev'ry day to be
Good and gentle, more like Thee.

Now the Light Has Gone Away, st. 2

Luther's Evening Prayer

I thank You, my heavenly Father, through Jesus Christ, Your dear Son, that You have graciously kept me this day; and I pray that You would forgive me all my sins where I have done wrong, and graciously keep me this night. For into Your hands I commend myself, my body and soul, and all things. Let Your holy angel be with me, that the evil foe may have no power over me. Amen.

Confession and Absolution

In the name of the Father and of the ✠ Son and
of the Holy Spirit.
Amen.

Beloved in the Lord! Let us draw near with a true heart and
confess our sins unto God our Father, asking Him in the name
of our Lord Jesus Christ to grant us forgiveness.

Our help is in the name of the Lord,
who made heaven and earth.

I said, I will confess my sins to the Lord,
and You forgave my sin.

Almighty God, our maker and redeemer, we poor
sinners confess unto You that we are by nature sinful and
unclean and that we have sinned against You by thought,
word, and deed. Wherefore we flee for refuge to Your infinite
mercy, seeking and imploring Your grace for the sake of our
Lord Jesus Christ.

Family members may confess their sins to one another.

O most merciful God, who has given Your only-begotten Son to die for us, have mercy upon us and for His sake grant us forgiveness for all our sins; and by Your Holy Spirit increase in us true knowledge of You and of Your will and true obedience to Your Word, to the end that by Your grace we may come to everlasting life; through Jesus Christ, our Lord. Amen.

Almighty God, our heavenly Father, has had mercy upon us and has given His only Son to die for us and for His sake forgives us all our sins.

Let us bless the Lord.
Thanks be to God.

Apostles' Creed

**I believe in God, the Father Almighty,
maker of heaven and earth.**

And in Jesus Christ, His only Son, our Lord,
who was conceived by the Holy Spirit,
born of the virgin Mary,
suffered under Pontius Pilate,
was crucified, died and was buried.
He descended into hell.
The third day He rose again from the dead.
He ascended into heaven
and sits at the right hand of God the Father Almighty.
From thence He will come to judge
the living and the dead.

I believe in the Holy Spirit,
   the holy Christian Church,
     the communion of saints,
   the forgiveness of sins,
   the resurrection of the body,
   and the life ✣ everlasting. Amen.

The Lord's Prayer

Our Father who art in heaven,
   hallowed be Thy name,
   Thy kingdom come,
   Thy will be done on earth
       as it is in heaven;
   give us this day our daily bread;
   and forgive us our trespasses
       as we forgive those
       who trespass against us;
   and lead us not into temptation,
   but deliver us from evil.
For Thine is the kingdom
   and the power and the glory
   forever and ever. Amen.

The Advent of Our King

1 The ad - vent of our King Our
2 All glo - ry to the Son, Who

prayers must now em - ploy,
comes to set us free,

And we must hymns of wel - come sing In
With Fa - ther, Spir - it, ev - er one Through

strains of ho - ly joy.
all e - ter - ni - ty.

On Jordan's Bank the Baptist's Cry

1 On Jor - dan's bank the Bap - tist's cry An - nounc - es
2 All praise, e - ter - nal Son, to Thee Whose ad - vent

that the Lord is nigh; A - wake and hear - ken,
sets Thy peo - ple free, Whom with the Fa - ther

for he brings Glad tid - ings of the King of kings!
we a - dore And Ho - ly Spir - it ev - er - more.

Savior of the Nations, Come

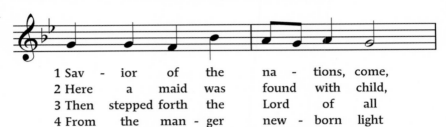

1 Sav - ior of the na - tions, come,
2 Here a maid was found with child,
3 Then stepped forth the Lord of all
4 From the man - ger new - born light

Vir - gin's Son, make here Your home!
Yet re - mained a vir - gin mild.
From His pure and king - ly hall;
Shines in glo - ry through the night.

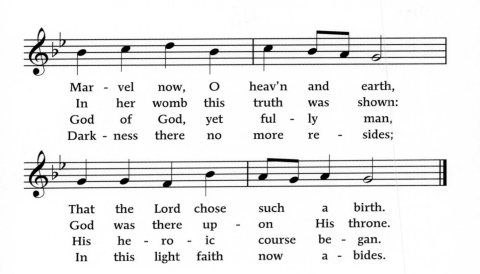

Mar - vel now, O heav'n and earth,
In her womb this truth was shown:
God of God, yet ful - ly man,
Dark - ness there no more re - sides;

That the Lord chose such a birth.
God was there up - on His throne.
His he - ro - ic course be - gan.
In this light faith now a - bides.

O Come, O Come, Emmanuel

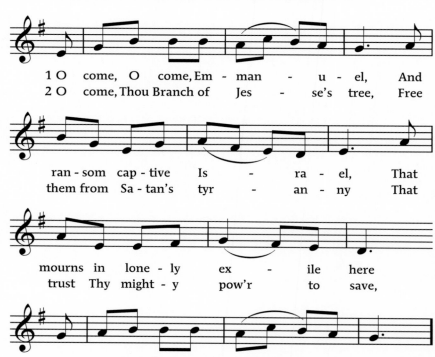

1 O come, O come, Em - man - u - el, And
2 O come, Thou Branch of Jes - se's tree, Free

ran - som cap - tive Is - ra - el, That
them from Sa - tan's tyr - an - ny That

mourns in lone - ly ex - ile here
trust Thy might - y pow'r to save,

Un - til the Son of God ap - pear.
And give them vic - t'ry o'er the grave.

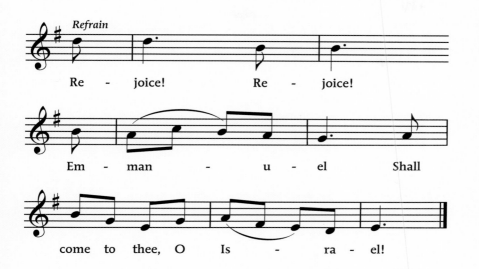

Refrain

Re - joice! Re - joice! Em - man - u - el Shall come to thee, O Is - ra - el!

From Heaven Above to Earth I Come

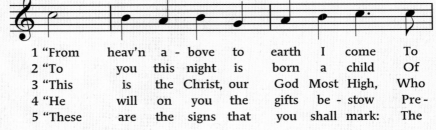

1 "From   heav'n a - bove to   earth   I   come   To
2 "To   you   this night is   born   a   child   Of
3 "This   is   the   Christ, our   God Most High,   Who
4 "He   will   on   you   the   gifts be - stow   Pre -
5 "These   are   the   signs that you shall mark: The

bear   good   news   to   ev - 'ry   home;   Glad
Mar - y,   cho - sen   vir - gin   mild;   This
hears   your   sad   and   bit - ter   cry;   He
pared   by   God   for   all   be - low,   That
swad - dling clothes and   man - ger dark.   There

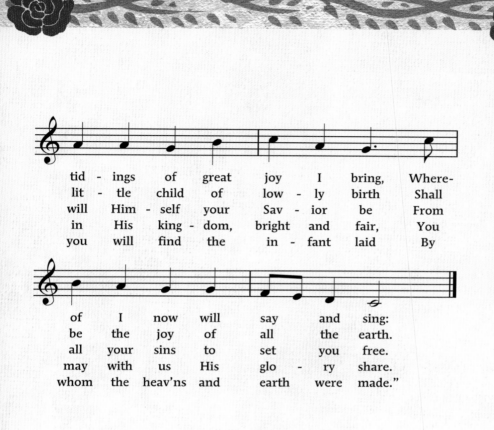

tid - ings of great joy I bring, Where-
lit - tle child of low - ly birth Shall
will Him - self your Sav - ior be From
in His king - dom, bright and fair, You
you will find the in - fant laid By

of I now will say and sing:
be the joy of all the earth.
all your sins to set you free.
may with us His glo - ry share.
whom the heav'ns and earth were made."

Silent Night, Holy Night

1 Si - lent night, ho - ly night! All is calm,
2 Si - lent night, ho - ly night! Shep-herds quake
3 Si - lent night, ho - ly night! Son of God,

all is bright Round yon vir - gin moth-er and child.
at the sight; Glo - ries stream from heav-en a - far,
love's pure light Ra - diant beams from Thy ho - ly face

Ho - ly In-fant, so ten-der and mild, Sleep in heav-en-ly
Heav'n-ly hosts sing, Al - le - lu - ia! Christ, the Sav-ior, is
With the dawn of re - deem - ing grace, Je - sus, Lord, at Thy

peace, Sleep in heav - en - ly peace.
born! Christ, the Sav - ior, is born!
birth, Je - sus, Lord, at Thy birth.

Away in a Manger

1 A - way in a man - ger, no crib for a bed,
2 The cat - tle are low - ing, the ba - by a - wakes,
3 Be near me, Lord Je - sus; I ask Thee to stay

The lit - tle Lord Je - sus laid down His sweet head.
But lit - tle Lord Je - sus, no cry - ing He makes.
Close by me for - ev - er and love me, I pray.

The stars in the sky____ looked down where He lay,
I love Thee, Lord Je - sus! Look down from the sky,
Bless all the dear chil - dren in Thy ten - der care,

The lit - tle Lord Je - sus a - sleep on the hay.
And stay by my cra - dle till morn - ing is nigh.
And take us to heav - en to live with Thee there.

O Come, Little Children

1 O come, lit - tle chil - dren, O
2 He's born in a sta - ble for
3 See Mar - y and Jo - seph, with
4 Kneel down and a - dore Him with

come, one and all, To Beth - le - hem
you and for me; Draw near by the
love - beam-ing eyes, Are gaz - ing up -
shep - herds to - day, Lift up lit - tle

haste to the man - ger so small. God's
bright, gleam-ing star - light to see, In
on the rude bed where He lies; The
hands now and praise Him as they; Re -

Son for a gift has been sent you this
swad - dling clothes ly - ing, so meek and so
shep - herds are kneel - ing, with hearts full of
joice that a Sav - ior from sin you can

night To be your Re - deem - er, your
mild, And pur - er than an - gels, the
love, While an - gels sing loud al - le -
boast, And join in the song of the

Joy, and De - light.
heav - en - ly child.
lu - ias a - bove.
heav - en - ly host.

Angels We Have Heard on High

1 An - gels we have heard on high,
2 Shep - herds, why this ju - bi - lee?
3 Come to Beth - le - hem and see

Sweet - ly sing - ing o'er the plains,
Why your joy - ous strains pro - long?
Him whose birth the an - gels sing;

And the moun - tains in re - ply,
What the glad - some tid - ings be
Come, a - dore on bend - ed knee

Ech - o - ing their joy - ous strains.
Which in - spire your heav'n - ly song?
Christ the Lord, the new - born King.

God Loves Me Dearly

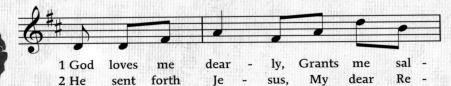

1 God loves me dear - ly, Grants me sal -
2 He sent forth Je - sus, My dear Re -
3 Je - sus, my Sav - ior, Him - self did

va - tion, God loves me dear - ly, Loves e - ven me.
deem - er, He sent forth Je - sus And set me free.
of - fer; Je - sus, my Sav - ior, Paid all I owed.

52

There - fore I'll say a - gain: God loves me

dear - ly, God loves me dear - ly, Loves e - ven me.

As with Gladness Men of Old

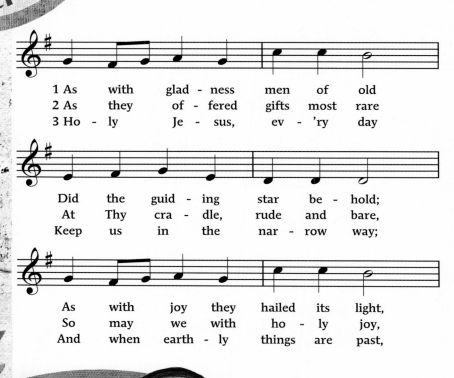

1 As with glad - ness men of old
2 As they of - fered gifts most rare
3 Ho - ly Je - sus, ev - 'ry day

Did the guid - ing star be - hold;
At Thy cra - dle, rude and bare,
Keep us in the nar - row way;

As with joy they hailed its light,
So may we with ho - ly joy,
And when earth - ly things are past,

Lead - ing on - ward, beam - ing bright;
Pure and free from sin's al - loy,
Bring our ran - somed souls at last

So, most gra - cious Lord, may we
All our cost - liest trea - sures bring,
Where they need no star to guide,

Ev - er - more be led by Thee.
Christ, to Thee, our heav'n - ly King.
Where no clouds Thy glo - ry hide.

I Want to Walk as a Child of the Light

1 I want to walk as a child of the light.
2 I want to see the bright-ness of God.
3 I'm look-ing for the com-ing of Christ.

I want to fol - low Je - sus.
I want to look at Je - sus.
I want to be with Je - sus.

God set the stars to give light to the world.
Clear Sun of Righ-teous-ness, shine on my path,
When we have run with pa-tience the race,

The star of my life is Je - sus.
And show me the way to the Fa - ther.
We shall know the joy of Je - sus.

Refrain

In Him there is no dark-ness at all.

The night and the day are both a-like.

The Lamb is the light of the cit-y of God.

Shine in my heart, Lord Je - sus.

57

O Lord, throughout These Forty Days

1 O Lord, through-out these for-ty days You
2 Be with us through this sea-son, Lord, And

prayed and kept the fast; In - spire re - pen-tance
all our earth-ly days, That when the fi - nal

for our sin, And free us from our past.
Eas - ter dawns, We join in heav-en's praise.

On My Heart Imprint Your Image

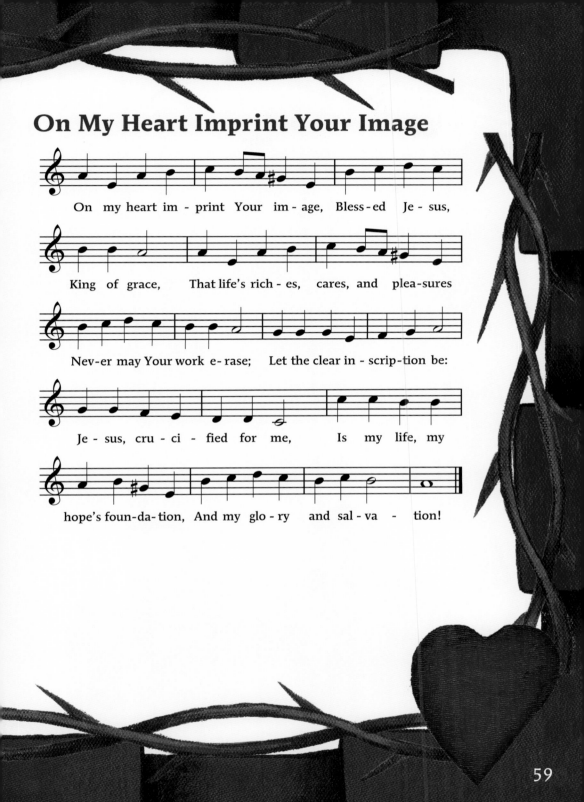

On my heart im - print Your im - age, Bless - ed Je - sus,
King of grace, That life's rich - es, cares, and plea-sures
Nev - er may Your work e - rase; Let the clear in - scrip-tion be:
Je - sus, cru - ci - fied for me, Is my life, my
hope's foun-da-tion, And my glo - ry and sal - va - tion!

Glory Be to Jesus

1 Glo - ry be to Je - sus,
2 Grace and life e - ter - nal
3 Oft as earth ex - ult - ing
4 Lift we, then, our voic - es,

Who in bit - ter pains   Poured for me the
In that blood I find;   Blest be His com -
Wafts its praise on high,   An - gel hosts re -
Swell the might - y flood;   Loud - er still and

life - blood   From His sa - cred veins!
pas - sion,   In - fi - nite - ly kind!
joic - ing   Make their glad re - ply.
loud - er   Praise the pre - cious blood!

All Glory, Laud, and Honor

Refrain

All glo - ry, laud, and hon - or To

You, Re - deem - er, King, To whom the lips of

chil - dren Made sweet ho - san - nas ring.

1 You are the King of Is - rael And
2 The com - pa - ny of an - gels Is
3 As You re - ceived their prais - es, Ac -

Da - vid's roy - al Son, Now in the Lord's name
prais - ing You on high, And we with all cre -
cept the prayers we bring, O Source of ev - 'ry

Refrain

com - ing, Our King and Bless - ed One.
a - tion In cho - rus make re - ply.
bless - ing, Our good and gra - cious King.

What Is This Bread

1 What is this bread?   Christ's bod - y
2 What is this wine?   The blood of
3 So who am I,   That I should
4 Yet is God here?   Oh, yes! By
5 Is this for me?   I am for -

ris - en from the dead: This bread we break,
Je - sus shed for mine;   The cup of grace
live and He should die   Un - der the rod?
Word and prom - ise clear,   In mouth and soul
giv - en and set free!   I do be - lieve

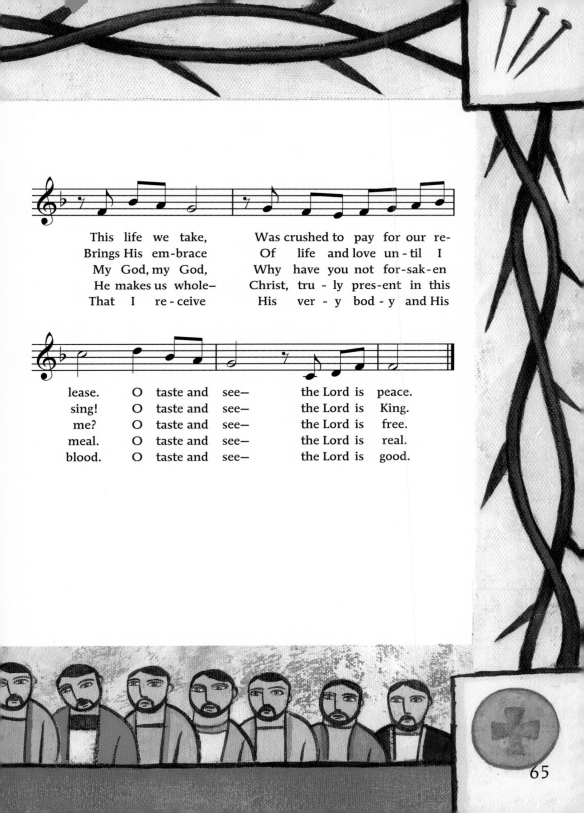

This life we take,   Was crushed to pay for our re-
Brings His em-brace   Of life and love un-til I
My God, my God,   Why have you not for-sak-en
He makes us whole–   Christ, tru-ly pres-ent in this
That I re-ceive   His ver-y bod-y and His

lease.   O taste and see—   the Lord is peace.
sing!   O taste and see—   the Lord is King.
me?   O taste and see—   the Lord is free.
meal.   O taste and see—   the Lord is real.
blood.   O taste and see—   the Lord is good.

Go to Dark Gethsemane

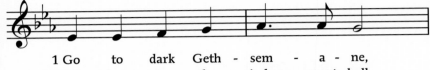

1 Go to dark Geth - sem - a - ne,
2 Fol - low to the judg - ment hall,
3 Cal - v'ry's mourn - ful moun - tain climb;
4 Ear - ly has - ten to the tomb

All who feel the tempt - er's pow'r;
View the Lord of life ar - raigned;
There, a - dor - ing at His feet,
Where they laid His breath - less clay;

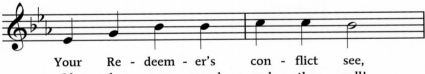

Your Re - deem - er's con - flict see,
Oh, the worm - wood and the gall!
Mark that mir - a - cle of time,
All is sol - i - tude and gloom.

Watch with Him one bit - ter hour;
Oh, the pangs His soul sus - tained!
God's own sac - ri - fice com - plete.
Who has tak - en Him a - way?

Turn not from His griefs a - way;
Shun not suf - f'ring, shame, or loss;
"It is fin - ished!" hear Him cry;
Christ is ris'n! He meets our eyes.

Learn from Je - sus Christ to pray.
Learn from Him to bear the cross.
Learn from Je - sus Christ to die.
Sav - ior, teach us so to rise.

67

The Lamb

1 The Lamb, the Lamb, O
2 The Lamb, the Lamb, One
3 The Lamb, the Lamb, As
4 He sighs, He dies, He

Fa - ther, where's the sac - ri - fice? Faith sees, be -
per - fect fi - nal of - fer - ing. The Lamb, the
way - ward sheep their shep - herd kill So still, His
takes my sin and wretch - ed - ness. He lives, for -

lieves God will pro - vide the Lamb of price!
Lamb, Let earth join heav'n His praise to sing.
will On our be - half the Law to fill.
gives, He gives me His own righ - teous - ness.

Refrain

Wor-thy is the Lamb whose death makes me His own! The Lamb is reign-ing on His throne!

69

Lamb of God

Lamb of God, You take a-way the sin of the world; have

mer-cy on us. Lamb of God, You take a-way the sin of the

world; have mer-cy on us. Lamb of God, You take a-way the

sin of the world; grant us peace.

Jesus Christ Is Risen Today

1 Je - sus Christ is ris'n to - day,
2 Hymns of praise then let us sing,
3 But the pains which He en - dured,
4 Sing we to our God a - bove,

Al - le - lu - ia!

Our tri - um - phant ho - ly day,
Un - to Christ, our heav'n - ly king,
Our sal - va - tion have pro - cured;
Praise e - ter - nal as His love;

Al - le - lu - ia!

Who did once up - on the cross,
Who en - dured the cross and grave,
Now a - bove the sky He's king,
Praise Him, all ye heav'n - ly host,

Al - - le - lu - ia!

Suf - fer to re - deem our loss.
Sin - ners to re - deem and save.
Where the an - gels ev - er sing.
Fa - ther, Son, and Ho - ly Ghost.

Al - - le - lu - ia!

I Know That My Redeemer Lives

1 I know that my Re - deem - er
2 He lives to bless me with His
3 He lives to si - lence all my
4 He lives, my kind, wise, heav'n - ly

lives; What com - fort this sweet sen - tence
love; He lives to plead for me a -
fears; He lives to wipe a - way my
friend; He lives and loves me to the

gives! He lives, He lives, who
bove; He lives my hun - gry
tears; He lives to calm my
end; He lives, and while He

74

once   was   dead;   He   lives, my
soul   to   feed;   He   lives   to
trou - bled   heart;   He   lives   all
lives,   I'll   sing;   He   lives, my

ev - er - liv - ing   head.
help   in   time   of   need.
bless - ings   to   im - part.
Proph - et,   Priest,   and   King.

Holy Spirit, Light Divine

1 Ho - ly Spir - it, light di - vine, Shine up - on this
2 Let me see my Sav - ior's face, Let me all His
3 Ho - ly Spir - it, pow'r di - vine, Cleanse this guilt - y
4 Ho - ly Spir - it, joy di - vine, Cheer this sad - dened
5 Ho - ly Spir - it, all di - vine, Dwell with - in this

heart of mine; Chase the shades of night a - way,
beau - ties trace; Show those glo - rious truths to me
heart of mine; In Thy mer - cy pit - y me,
heart of mine; Yield a sa - cred, set - tled peace,
heart of mine; Cast down ev - 'ry i - dol throne,

Turn the dark - ness in - to day.
Which are on - ly known to Thee.
From sin's bond - age set me free.
Let it grow and still in - crease.
Reign su - preme, and reign a - lone.

Holy, Holy, Holy

1 Ho - ly, ho - ly, ho - ly!
2 Ho - ly, ho - ly, ho - ly!
3 Ho - ly, ho - ly, ho - ly!
4 Ho - ly, ho - ly, ho - ly!

Lord____ God Al - might - y!
All the saints a - dore Thee,
Though the dark - ness hide Thee,
Lord____ God Al - might - y!

Ear - ly in the morn - ing our
Cast - ing down their gold - en crowns a -
Though the eye of sin - ful man Thy
All Thy works shall praise Thy name in

song shall rise to Thee;
round the glass - y sea;
glo - ry may not see,
earth and sky and sea.

Ho - ly, ho - ly, ho - ly,
Cher - u - bim and ser - a - phim
On - ly Thou art ho - ly;
Ho - ly, ho - ly, ho - ly,

mer - ci - ful and might - y!
fall - ing down be - fore Thee,
there is none be - side Thee,
mer - ci - ful and might - y!

God in three per - sons,
Which wert and art and
Per - fect in pow'r, in
God in three per - sons,

bless - ed Trin - i - ty!
ev - er - more shalt be.
love, and pu - ri - ty.
bless - ed Trin - i - ty!

Someone Special

1 Some - one Spe - cial, I know who:
2 Some - one Spe - cial, that You are,
3 Some - one Spe - cial, who would give
4 Some - one Spe - cial, who would send
5 Some - one Spe - cial— God and man,

That Some - one, my God, is You!
To cre - ate the Christ - mas Star,
His own Son that all might live,
His good Spir - it for a Friend,
You were there when I be - gan,

Who could make a world like this
Her - ald - ing the Sav - ior's birth,
And by Him would set us free
Faith Cre - a - tor, Light and Guide,
You'll be there when I de - part,

And a heav - en full of bliss;
Bring - ing peace and joy to earth.
From all sin and mis - er - y.
Al - ways stand - ing at my side.
For You live with - in my heart.

Some - one spe - cial I must be,
Some - one spe - cial I must be,
Some - one spe - cial I must be,
Some - one spe - cial I must be,
Some - one spe - cial— now I see,

Since You made it all for me!
Since You made that Star for me!
Since You gave Your Son for me!
Since You gave that Gift to me!
That some - one is real - ly me.

Beautiful Savior

1 Beau - ti - ful   Sav - ior,   King   of   cre -
2 Fair   are   the   mead - ows,   Fair   are   the
3 Fair   is   the   sun - shine,   Fair   is   the
4 Beau - ti - ful   Sav - ior,   Lord   of   the

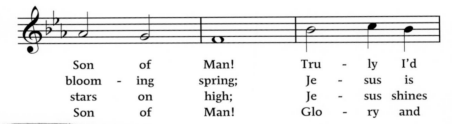

a - tion,   Son   of   God   and
wood - lands,   Robed   in   flow'rs   of
moon - light,   Bright   the   spar - kling
na - tions,   Son   of   God   and

Son   of   Man!   Tru - ly   I'd
bloom - ing   spring;   Je - sus   is
stars   on   high;   Je - sus   shines
Son   of   Man!   Glo - ry   and

82

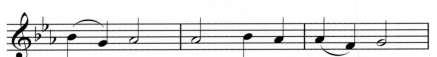

love Thee, Tru – ly I'd serve Thee,
fair – er, Je – sus is pur – er,
bright – er, Je – sus shines pur – er
hon – or, Praise, ad – o – ra – tion

Light of my soul, my joy, my crown.
He makes our sor – r'wing spir – it sing.
Than all the an – gels in the sky.
Now and for – ev – er – more be Thine!

Jesus Loves Me

1 Je - sus loves me! This I know,
2 Je - sus loves me! He who died

For the Bi - ble tells me so. Lit - tle ones to
Heav-en's gates to o - pen wide. He has washed a -

Him be - long; They are weak, but He is strong.
way my sin, Lets His lit - tle child come in.

Refrain

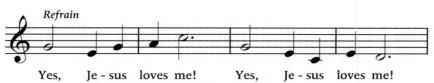

Yes, Je - sus loves me! Yes, Je - sus loves me!

Yes, Je - sus loves me! The Bi - ble tells me so.

The King of Love My Shepherd Is

1 The King of love my shep - herd
2 Where streams of liv - ing wa - ter
3 In death's dark vale I fear no
4 And so through all the length of

is, Whose good - ness fail - eth
flow, My ran - somed soul He
ill With Thee, dear Lord, be -
days Thy good - ness fail - eth

nev - er; I noth - ing
lead - eth And, where the
side me, Thy rod and
nev - er; Good Shep - herd,

lack   if   I   am   His   And
ver - dant   pas - tures   grow,   With
staff   my   com - fort   still,   Thy
may   I   sing   Thy   praise   With -

He   is   mine   for - ev - er.
food   ce - les - tial   feed - eth.
cross   be - fore   to   guide - me.
in   Thy   house   for - ev - er!

What a Friend We Have in Jesus

1 What a friend we have in Je - sus,
2 Have we tri - als and temp - ta - tions?
3 Are we weak and heav - y lad - en,

All our sins and griefs to bear!
Is there trou - ble an - y - where?
Cum - bered with a load of care?

What a priv - i - lege to car - ry
We should nev - er be dis - cour - aged—
Pre - cious Sav - ior, still our ref - uge—

Ev - 'ry - thing to God in prayer!
Take it to the Lord in prayer.
Take it to the Lord in prayer.

Oh,   what peace we of - ten   for   -   feit;
Can   we find a friend so   faith   -   ful
Do   thy friends de - spise, for - sake   thee?

Oh,   what need - less pain we   bear—
Who   will all our sor - rows   share?
Take   it to the Lord in   prayer.

All   be - cause we do not   car   -   ry
Je - sus knows our ev - 'ry   weak   -   ness—
In   His arms He'll take and   shield   thee;

Ev - 'ry - thing to God in   prayer!
Take   it to the Lord in   prayer.
Thou   wilt find a sol - ace   there.

Lift High the Cross

Refrain

Lift high the cross, the love of Christ pro-claim Till

all the world a - dore His sa - cred name.

1 Come, Chris-tians, fol - low   where our Cap-tain trod,
2 All   new - born sol - diers   of   the Cru - ci - fied
3 O   Lord, once lift - ed   on   the glo-rious tree,
4 So   shall   our song of   tri -umph ev - er   be:

Refrain

Our   king   vic - to - rious, Christ, the Son of   God.
Bear   on   their brows the   seal of Him who   died.
As   Thou   hast   pro - mised, draw us all   to   Thee.
Praise   to   the   Cru - ci - fied   for vic - to - ry!

Christ Be My Leader

1 Christ be my Lead-er by night as by day;
2 Christ be my Teach-er in age as in youth,
3 Christ be my Sav-ior in calm as in strife;

Safe through the dark-ness, for He is the way.
Drift-ing or doubt-ing, for He is the truth.
Death can-not hold me, for He is the life. Nor

Glad-ly I fol-low, my fu-ture His care,
Grant me to trust Him; though shift-ing as sand,
dark-ness nor doubt-ing nor sin and its stain Can

Dark-ness is day-light when Je-sus is there.
Doubt can-not daunt me; in Je-sus I stand.
touch my sal - va - tion: with Je-sus I reign.

I Am Trusting Thee, Lord Jesus

1 I am trust - ing Thee, Lord Je - sus,
2 I am trust - ing Thee for par - don;
3 I am trust - ing Thee to guide me;
4 I am trust - ing Thee, Lord Je - sus;

Trust - ing on - ly Thee; Trust - ing Thee for
At Thy feet I bow, For Thy grace and
Thou a - lone shalt lead, Ev - 'ry day and
Nev - er let me fall. I am trust - ing

full sal - va - tion, Great and free.
ten - der mer - cy Trust - ing now.
hour sup - ply - ing All my need.
Thee for - ev - er And for all.

Thank the Lord

Thank the Lord and sing His praise;
tell ev - 'ry - one what He has done.
Let all who seek the Lord re -
joice and proud - ly bear His name.
He re - calls His prom - is - es and
leads His peo - ple forth in joy with
shouts of thanks-giv-ing. Al -le - lu - ia, al -le-lu - ia.

95

Have No Fear, Little Flock

1 Have   no   fear,   lit - tle   flock;   Have   no
2 Have   good   cheer,   lit - tle   flock;   Have   good
3 Praise   the   Lord   high   a - bove;   Praise   the
4 Thank - ful   hearts   raise   to   God;   Thank - ful

fear,   lit - tle flock, For the   Fa - ther has cho - sen To
cheer,   lit - tle flock, For the   Fa - ther will keep you In
Lord   high a - bove, For He stoops down to   heal you, Up-
hearts raise to   God, For He stays   close be - side you, In

give you   the King - dom; Have no   fear,   lit - tle flock!
His love   for - ev - er; Have good cheer, lit - tle flock!
lift and   re - store you; Praise the Lord high a - bove!
all things works with   you; Thank - ful hearts raise to   God!

Lord, Keep Us Steadfast in Your Word

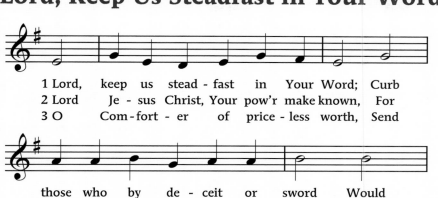

1 Lord, keep us stead-fast in Your Word; Curb
2 Lord Je-sus Christ, Your pow'r make known, For
3 O Com-fort-er of price-less worth, Send

those who by de-ceit or sword Would
You are Lord of lords a-lone; De-
peace and u-ni-ty on earth; Sup-

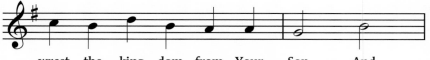

wrest the king-dom from Your Son And
fend Your ho-ly Church that we May
port us in our fi-nal strife And

bring to naught all He has done.
sing Your praise e-ter-nal-ly.
lead us out of death to life.

A Mighty Fortress Is Our God

1 A might - y for - tress is our God,
2 With might of ours can naught be done,

A trust - y shield and weap - on;
Soon were our loss ef - fect - ed;

He helps us free from ev - 'ry need
But for us fights the val - iant One,

That hath us now o'er - tak - en.
Whom God Him - self e - lect - ed.

The old e - vil foe
Ask ye, Who is this?

Now means dead - ly woe; Deep guile and
Je - sus Christ it is, Of Sab - a -

great might Are his dread arms in fight;
oth Lord, And there's none oth - er God;

On earth is not his e - qual.
He holds the field for - ev - er.

Amazing Grace

1 A - maz - ing grace— how sweet the
2 The Lord has prom - ised good to

sound— That saved a wretch like me!
me, His Word my hope se - cures;

I once was lost but now am
He will my shield and por - tion

found, Was blind but now I see!
be As long as life en - dures.

Praise God, from Whom All Blessings Flow

Praise God, from whom all bless - ings flow; Praise

Him, all crea - tures here be - low; Praise

Him a - bove, ye heav'n - ly host: Praise

Fa - ther, Son, and Ho - ly Ghost. A - men.

Praise to the Lord, the Almighty

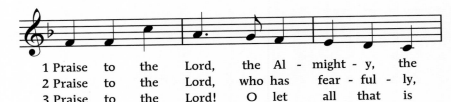

1 Praise to the Lord, the Al - might - y, the
2 Praise to the Lord, who has fear - ful - ly,
3 Praise to the Lord! O let all that is

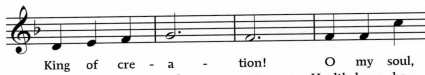

King of cre - a - tion! O my soul,
won-drous - ly, made you, Health has be -
in me a - dore Him! All that has

praise Him, for He is your health and sal -
stowed and, when heed - less - ly fall - ing, has
life and breath, come now with prais - es be -

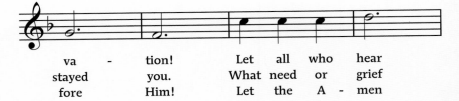

va - tion! Let all who hear
stayed you. What need or grief
fore Him! Let the A - men

Now to His tem - ple draw near,
Ev - er has failed of re - lief?
Sound from His peo - ple a - gain;

Join - ing in glad ad - o - ra - tion!
Wings of His mer - cy did shade you.
Glad - ly for - ev - er a - dore Him!

Now Thank We All Our God

1 Now thank we all our God With
2 Oh, may this boun-teous God Through
3 All praise and thanks to God The

hearts and hands and voic - es, Who won-drous things has
all our life be near us, With ev - er joy - ful
Fa - ther now be giv - en, The Son, and Him who

done, In whom His world re - joic - es;
hearts And bless - ed peace to cheer us
reigns With them in high - est heav - en,

Who from our moth - ers' arms Has
And keep us in His grace And
The one e - ter - nal God, Whom

blest us on our way With count-less gifts of
guide us when per - plexed And free us from all
earth and heav'n a - dore; For thus it was, is

love And still is ours to - day.
ills In this world and the next!
now, And shall be ev - er - more.

Now That the Daylight Fills the Sky

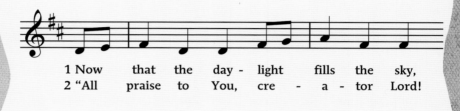

1 Now that the day - light fills the sky,
2 "All praise to You, cre - a - tor Lord!

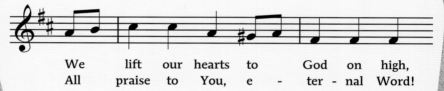

We lift our hearts to God on high,
All praise to You, e - ter - nal Word!

That He, in all we do or say,
All praise to You, O Spir - it wise!"

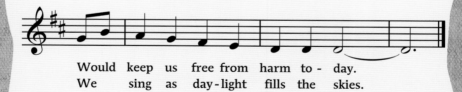

Would keep us free from harm to - day.
We sing as day - light fills the skies.

Abide with Me

1 A - bide with me, fast falls the e - ven - tide.
2 I need Thy pres - ence ev - 'ry pass - ing hour;
3 I fear no foe with Thee at hand to bless;
4 Hold Thou Thy cross be - fore my clos - ing eyes;

The dark - ness deep - ens; Lord, with me a - bide.
What but Thy grace can foil the tempt - er's pow'r?
Ills have no weight and tears no bit - ter - ness.
Shine through the gloom, and point me to the skies.

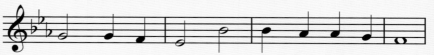

When oth - er help - ers fail and com - forts flee,
Who like Thy - self my guide and stay can be?
Where is death's sting? Where, grave, thy vic - to - ry?
Heav'n's morn - ing breaks, and earth's vain shad - ows flee;

Help of the help - less, O a - bide with me.
Through cloud and sun - shine, O a - bide with me.
I tri - umph still if Thou a - bide with me!
In life, in death, O Lord, a - bide with me.

This Is the Feast

Refrain

This is the feast of vic-to-ry for our God.

Al-le-lu-ia, al-le-lu-ia, al-le-lu-ia.

Wor-thy is Christ, the Lamb who was slain, whose

Refrain

blood set us free to be peo-ple of God.

See This Wonder in the Making

1 See this won-der in the mak-ing: God Him-
2 Mir-a-cle each time it hap-pens As the
3 Far more ten-der than a moth-er, Far more
4 Here we bring a child of na-ture; Home we

self this child is tak-ing As a
door to heav-en o-pens And the
car-ing than a fa-ther, God, in -
take a new-born crea-ture, Now God's

lamb safe in His keep-ing, His to
Fa-ther beams, "Be-lov-ed, Heir of
to Your arms we place *him/her/them,* With Your
pre-cious son or daugh-ter, Born a-

be, a-wake or sleep-ing.
gifts a king would cov-et!"
love and peace em-brace *him/her/them.*
gain by Word and wa-ter.

Cling Tightly to the Word of God

1 Cling tight - ly to the Word of God And
2 Re - call in faith the pre - cious gift Of

Christ's dis - ci - ple be; For
your bap - tis - mal day, When

then, be - lov - ed, you will know The
you were joined to Je - sus' death That

truth that sets you free, The
washed your sins a - way, That

truth that sets you free.
washed your sins a - way.

Baptized into Your Name Most Holy

1 Bap - tized in - to Your name most
2 All that I am and love most

ho - ly, O Fa - ther, Son, and Ho - ly
dear - ly— Re - ceive it all, O Lord, from

Ghost, I claim a place, though weak and
me. Let me con - fess my faith sin -

low - ly, A - mong Your saints, Your cho - sen
cere - ly; Help me Your faith - ful child to

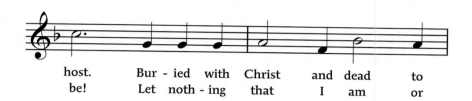

host.   Bur - ied with Christ   and dead   to
be!   Let noth - ing that   I am   or

sin,   Your Spir - it now   shall live   with - in.
own   Serve an - y will   but Yours   a - lone.

115

Father Welcomes

Refrain

Fa - ther wel-comes all His chil-dren To His fam -'ly

through His Son. Fa - ther giv - ing His sal - va - tion,

Life for - ev - er has been won.

1 Lit - tle chil - dren, come to Me, For My king - dom
2 In the wa - ter, in the Word, In His prom - ise,
3 Let us dai - ly die to sin; Let us dai - ly

is of these. Life and___ love I have to give,
be as - sured: Those who are bap-tized and be - lieve
rise with Him, Walk in the love of Christ our Lord,

Refrain

Mer - cy___ for your sin.
Shall be___ born a - gain.
Live in the peace of God.

God's Own Child, I Gladly Say It

1 God's own child, I glad - ly say it:
2 Sa - tan, hear this proc - la - ma - tion:
3 There is noth - ing worth com - par - ing

I am bap - tized in - to Christ!
I am bap - tized in - to Christ!
To this life - long com - fort sure!

He, be - cause I could not pay it,
Drop your ug - ly ac - cu - sa - tion,
O - pen - eyed my grave is star - ing:

Gave my full re - demp - tion price.
I am not so soon en - ticed.
E - ven there I'll sleep se - cure.

Do I need earth's trea - sures man - y?
Now that to the font I've trav - eled,
Though my flesh a - waits its rais - ing,

I have one worth more than an - y
All your might has come un - rav - eled,
Still my soul con - tin - ues prais - ing:

That brought me sal - va - tion free
And, a - gainst your tyr - an - ny,
I am bap - tized in - to Christ;

Last - ing to e - ter - ni - ty!
God, my Lord, u - nites with me!
I'm a child of par - a - dise!

Go, My Children, with My Blessing

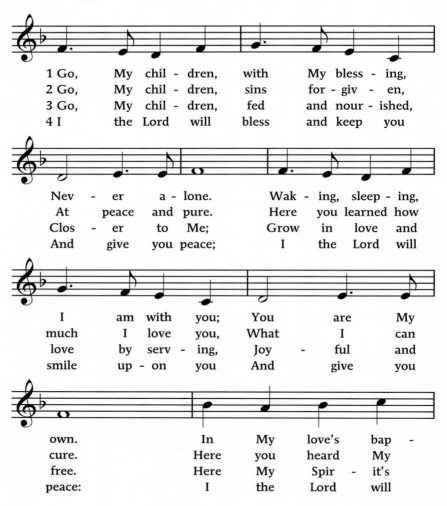

1 Go, My chil - dren, with My bless - ing,
2 Go, My chil - dren, sins for - giv - en,
3 Go, My chil - dren, fed and nour - ished,
4 I the Lord will bless and keep you

Nev - er a - lone. Wak - ing, sleep - ing,
At peace and pure. Here you learned how
Clos - er to Me; Grow in love and
And give you peace; I the Lord will

I am with you; You are My
much I love you, What I can
love by serv - ing, Joy - ful and
smile up - on you And give you

own. In My love's bap -
cure. Here My you heard My
free. Here My Spir - it's
peace: I the Lord will

tis - mal riv - er   I have made you
dear Son's sto - ry;   Here you touched Him,
pow - er filled you;   Here His ten - der
be your Fa - ther,   Sav - ior, Com - fort -

Mine   for - ev - er.   Go, My chil - dren,
saw   His glo - ry.   Go, My chil - dren,
com - fort stilled you. Go, My chil - dren,
er,   and Broth - er.   Go, My chil - dren;

with   My bless - ing— You are My own.
sins   for - giv - en,   At   peace and pure.
fed   and nour - ished, Joy - ful and free.
I   will keep you   And give you peace.

Children of the Heavenly Father

1 Chil - dren of the heav'n-ly Fa - ther Safe - ly
2 God His own doth tend and nour - ish; In His
3 Nei - ther life nor death shall ev - er From the
4 Though He giv - eth or He tak - eth, God His

in His bos - om gath - er; Nest-ling bird nor star in
ho - ly courts they flour-ish. From all e - vil things He
Lord His chil - dren sev - er; Un - to them His grace He
chil-dren ne'er for - sak - eth; His the lov - ing pur-pose

heav - en Such a ref - uge e'er was giv - en.
spares them; In His might - y arms He bears them.
show - eth, And their sor - rows all He know - eth.
sole - ly To pre - serve them pure and ho - ly.

I Am Jesus' Little Lamb

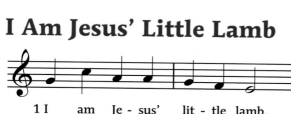

1 I am Je - sus' lit - tle lamb, Ev - er glad at
2 Day by day, at home, a - way, Je - sus is my
3 Who so hap - py as I am, E - ven now the

heart I am; For my Shep - herd gent-ly guides me,
staff and stay. When I hun - ger, Je - sus feeds me,
Shep - herd's lamb? And when my short life is end - ed,

Knows my need and well pro - vides me, Loves me ev - 'ry
In - to pleas-ant pas-tures leads me; When I thirst, He
By His an - gel host at - tend - ed, He shall fold me

day the same, E - ven calls me by my name.
bids me go Where the qui - et wa - ters flow.
to His breast, There with - in His arms to rest.

Acknowledgments

Editorial—Nancy Adams, Jean Baue, David Johnson, Peter Reske

Artists—Tamara Bishop, Paine Proffitt

The liturgical material on pages 22–37 is covered by the copyright of this book.

The catechism translation is copyright © 1986 Concordia Publishing House.

"A Mighty Fortress Is Our God" **Text and tune:** Public domain

"Abide with Me" **Text and tune:** Public domain

"All Glory, Laud, and Honor" **Text and tune:** Public domain

"Amazing Grace" **Text and tune:** Public domain

"Angels We Have Heard on High" **Text and tune:** Public domain

"As with Gladness Men of Old" **Text and tune:** Public domain

"Away in a Manger" **Text and tune:** Public domain

"Baptized into Your Name Most Holy" **Text and tune:** Public domain

"Beautiful Savior" **Text and tune:** Public domain

"Children of the Heavenly Father" **Text:** © Board of Publications, Lutheran Church in America, admin. Augsburg Fortress. Reproduced by permission. **Tune:** Public domain

"Christ Be My Leader" **Text:** Timothy Dudley-Smith © 1964, ren. 1992 Hope Publishing Company, Carol Stream, IL 60188. All rights reserved. Used by permission. **Tune:** Public domain

"Cling Tightly to the Word of God" **Text:** © 2005 Stephen P. Starke, admin. Concordia Publishing House. **Tune:** © 2005 Wayne Leupold Editions, Inc. Used by permission.

"Father Welcomes" **Text and tune:** © 1986 Kevin Mayhew Ltd. Used by permission. License number 114002/1

"From Heaven Above to Earth I Come" **Text and tune:** Public domain

"Glory Be to Jesus" **Text and tune:** Public domain

"Go, My Children, with My Blessing" **Text:** © 1983 Concordia Publishing House. **Tune:** Public domain

"Go to Dark Gethsemane" **Text and tune:** Public domain

"God Loves Me Dearly" **Text and tune:** Public domain

"God's Own Child, I Gladly Say It" **Text:** © 1991 Robert E. Voelker.

Tune: Public domain

"Have No Fear, Little Flock" **Text and tune:** © 1973 Concordia Publishing House

"Holy, Holy, Holy" **Text and tune:** Public domain

"Holy Spirit, Light Divine" **Text and tune:** Public domain

"I Am Jesus' Little Lamb" **Text and tune:** Public domain

"I Am Trusting Thee, Lord Jesus" **Text and tune:** Public domain

"I Know That My Redeemer Lives" **Text and tune:** Public domain

"I Want to Walk as a Child of the Light" **Text and tune:** © 1970, 1975 Celebration

"Jesus Christ Is Risen Today" **Text and tune:** Public domain

"Jesus Loves Me" **Text and tune:** Public domain

"Lamb of God" **Text:** English translations of Lamb of God © 1988 English Language Liturgical Consultation (ELLC). www.englishtexts.org. Used by permission. **Tune:** © 1978 *Lutheran Book of Worship*

"Lift High the Cross" **Text:** George W. Kitchin and Michael R. Newbolt, and **Tune:** Sydney H. Nicholson © 1974 Hope Publishing Company, Carol Stream, IL 60188. All rights reserved. Used by permission.

"Lord, Keep Us Steadfast in Your Word" **Text and tune:** Public domain

"Now Thank We All Our God" **Text and tune:** Public domain

"Now That the Daylight Fills the Sky" **Text:** Public domain. **Tune:** © Lutheran Church Press and Augsburg Publishing House. Used by permission of Augsburg Fortress

"O Come, Little Children" **Text and tune:** Public domain

"O Come, O Come Emmanuel" **Text and tune:** Public domain

"O Lord, throughout These Forty Days" **Text:** © 1978 *Lutheran Book of Worship*. **Tune:** Public domain

"On Jordan's Bank the Baptist's Cry" **Text and tune:** Public domain

"On My Heart Imprint Your Image" **Text and tune:** Public domain

"Praise God, from Whom All Blessings Flow" **Text and tune:** Public domain

"Praise to the Lord, the Almighty" **Text and tune:** Public domain

"Savior of the Nations, Come" **Text:** St. 1: Public domain; sts. 2–4: © 1978, 2006 Concordia Publishing House. **Tune:** Public domain

"See This Wonder in the Making" **Text:** © 1984 Concordia Publishing House. **Tune:** Public domain

"Silent Night, Holy Night" **Text and tune:** Public domain

First Line Index

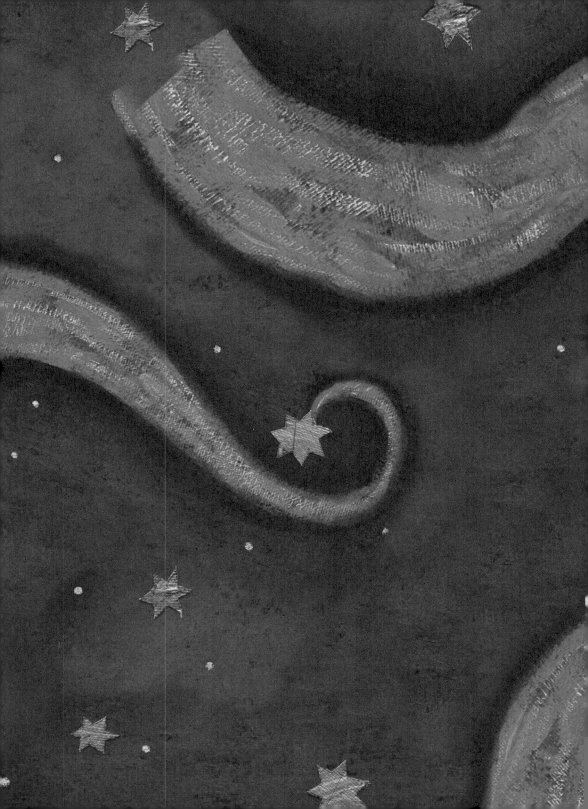